Journey to Healing: By God's Hands

Kearsen Danielle

MEADOWFUL LIGHT

ISBN: 979-8-9894457-1-4

Published in the United States by Meadowful Light.

Third Edition 2024

Kearsendanielle.com

To you,

The Lord hears you.
He sees you.
He knows you.
He is comforting you.
And He will save you.

*"The Lord is close to the brokenhearted and saves those who
are crushed in spirit."
Psalm 34:18*

Important Note From The Author

Often, when we go through a painful experience, we are left with some form of aftermath that is usually just as harsh, if not more. It can be hard to face and navigate that trauma in hopes of healing, especially if you're trying to do it alone.

The poems in this book follow the journey I began, not only to find healing but to find it in growing closer to God.

Piece by piece, I sat with the Lord to confront the experiences that had left me so broken. Doing this was hard. I had to take it slowly and be patient with myself. And through it all, I prayed and wrote so that maybe it would help someone else.

The first section, Brokenhearted Captive, contains poems portraying the confrontation of pain. At this point, I knew *of* God but did not know *Him*. And still, I called out and sat with Him as I faced the parts of my past that still haunted me. This section may be difficult for some to read and that is okay, however, it is a necessary step in your own journey. Facing, feeling, and releasing it. Remember to take care of yourself and be kind to your emotions, reactions, and process as a whole. Reach out for help should you need it. And most importantly, seek God through it all. He will give you strength, comfort, and rest.

In the next section, Beauty In Ashes, you will see the transformative part of the journey from not knowing Him to the renewing of the mind in surrendering. It is in the surrendering that you find who He truly is and grow that deeper relationship with Him.

Finally, you will find the Blossomed Branches section. Here, you'll see how surrendering and finding the Lord will change you. You should know that in beginning this journey with Him, you are not the same person and will not be the same person coming out of it that you were going in. When you start to heal with God, you're letting go of those broken pieces and allowing Him to mold you into who He created you to be.

Remember to be patient with yourself and know that no matter where you are in your process, even if you haven't started it, you are loved and God is comforting you. It is possible for you to find healing with Him.

In the second and third sections, there will be referenced scriptures at the end of each poem. The version being referenced throughout this book will be the New International Version (NIV).

Trigger Warning

Please take the time to look through these sensitive topics before beginning.

Sexual Abuse
Child Rape
Physical Abuse
Depression
Abandonment
Manipulation
Miscarriage

Suicidal Tendencies
Self-Harm
Anxiety
Infidelity
Substance Abuse
Toxic Relationships
Orphaned

Contents

BROKENHEARTED CAPTIVE

Journey to Healing

I watch as the lights quickly fade
Knowing all too well what is to follow
As pain slips under the door
I prepare for the cries I'll have to swallow
Every broken piece screaming from within
Aching to be heard
Simply needing a friend
But yet I am always alone
Faced with the darkness
That runs deep into my bones

Sirens scream in my ears
Awakening a part of myself I'd rather not exist
Bright lights filling my vision
The air in my chest struggling to move
Every bone shaking without force
My heart quakes repeatedly
Aching for help to keep beating
The voices of despair echoing around me

I am still here

Somehow I am balancing between worlds
Death strumming its guitar
Daring to cloud my head
And yet there's that part of me
The part that fights against it
Determined to live
Even with all the pain it entails

Journey to Healing

Pain overwhelms my body
Creeping along every inch
Grasping onto my skin for life
Digging its nails beneath the surface
Wrapping around my neck
Hungry for the air from my lungs
Desperate to be in control

To be felt
Or seen
To be heard

Drawing my inner self underneath its depths
Burying my soul within
Until I am all that it becomes
Wanting to be alive
In place of the person I once was

Kearsen Danielle

Silence forced onto me
Words wrapping around my mind
Tied to strings within your grasp

Consuming me

Pulling so roughly that I have no footing
No control over my thoughts
As the fear eats away at any hope
Keeping me trapped in this hell of a home
In this hell of a mind
Filled with so much darkness
Screaming at me every night

Buried beneath the ground
Enclosed in a casket of my greatest fears
I struggle to breathe through the cracks
My body becoming paralyzed
Mind running ragged
Endless thoughts fighting against another

The dirt knocks loudly above me
Desperate to creep inside
To soak up what's left of the air
While terror drips slowly into my lungs
Suffocating me from within
Sitting on my chest
Filling to the brim

Lips quivering
Breath shaking
Steadily quickening
The thoughts begin to scream
They know what is to come
From this darkening reality
But alas there is nothing left to save
For I've buried myself in this grave

Kearsen Danielle

The cold woke my mind
Jumping to connect with your hand
Squeezing around my throat
Struggling for the perfect fit
My body shivering beneath your touch
Afraid of what's to come
Vision fading into the dark
Your breath overwhelming my lungs
Smothering me completely
Every night
I lay drowning in your intoxication
While you lay on top of me

Glass shattering around her body
Screams consuming the air I breathe
Choking my heart with fear
Confusion
Misery
Time becoming a jumbled mess
Secretly spinning faster in the hope to save us
Nonetheless failing each time

As the blood trickles down
The fighting begins to flood over
Bodies trying to break through
Desperate to save us from the others
Hands carrying me into the dark
Trees stretching into the night sky

Further
Just a bit further
Until we are far from the lights
Far from the sirens produced
The trucks filling the drive
Fierce uniforms searching for me
Faces with that doleful look

Maybe they knew what was to come
Regardless
I was forever gone

Kearsen Danielle

Trapped inside these four walls
Fear eats at my consciousness
Building the knife inside my chest
Growing sharper
With each breath

There's no way out of this
The night is set to unravel before me
Once again I'm left to suffer
Or leave my body

Everything in sight becoming a blur
My words beg for him to stop
As his body hovers over mine
His arms like boulders against my own
Pushing harder against my cries

Soon I awake to his laugh
The pain rushing in like air itself
Overcoming every inch of my being
Voice catching in my throat
Afraid to be heard

Instead I lay paralyzed
Looking over myself
At the mess he left behind
The wreckage and death of an innocent soul
With no way to press rewind

Journey to Healing

The moonlight peeks through the blinds
Praying to get a glimpse that I'm alive

Unfortunately I am

Weakened by the monster inside
Bruised from my arms to my thighs
My soul has left this shattered mess
Watching from above as I lay undressed
Morning light may bring relief
But life will forever carry this grief
I've lost a part of myself I'll never get back
From a man that played the role of dad

Kearsen Danielle

I was just a toddler
A small innocent child when it all began
My life was supposed to be about ice cream and cartoons
Bicycles and holding hands

Instead

I spent my days walking on glass
Puncture after puncture
Hoping it would be the last
Only to find that the nights held worse
His rough hands that roamed too much
The alcohol that filled my lungs
Under his pressure I was crushed

Silent

Possible dead
As his body entered my own
I was just a child
Living with a monster in my home
My home
A place I should've felt safe
Yet no one could save me from his face
As he'd control my every breath underneath his hands
Squeeze too tightly and maybe it'll end

I just wanted to be safe in this home
Safe in this body

    a body that wasn't my own

Journey to Healing

The numbness has overcome
Snaking across my body
Latching onto my soul's core
Sucking my life to the last drop
Devoid of feeling
Not a care left for this world

It's almost freeing in a way
If it weren't so consuming
To be silent within
A vessel of pure emptiness
Slipping along until death
Until there's nothing left to exist

Kearsen Danielle

The air whispers to me at night
Sweetly singing all my fears
Mocking me with every note
Taking me back in time
To those moments in the dark
Drowning my mind

So I lay here for hours
Watching the shadows dance in my room
Silently praying none of them are you

Journey to Healing

I am a branch
    Broken and splintered
    Riddled with deep cuts
    Torn pieces from every tree I touched
    Never quite fitting
    But always sticking out
    An eyesore
    Something they'd rather be without

I am a branch
    Rough and imperfect
    A lonely branch
    Fallen
    Forgotten
    Left to wither away
    To crack and crumble
    Or perhaps to be tossed into the flames

Kearsen Danielle

There are strings tied to me
Pulling me behind you
Forcing me to bear witness to your destruction
Every drink that blinds you
Drowning your mind into submission
Are you too far to come back?

They don't tell you of the ones you hurt
The ones watching you wash away
Becoming but a shell upon the earth
Succumbing to the pain

My words scratch your skin…
　　　Mom, I need you.
Tugging at you with each step…
　　　How could you not see?
My cries fly like the birds…
　　　Why would you leave me?
Desperate to bring you joy…
　　　Wake up, please!
To make you stay…
　　　Do you even love me?

And yet your eyes sink beneath the clouds
Drifting into the quiet night without a sound

Was there ever anything to save?

Journey to Healing

Hands surround my body
Close but never touching
Constantly just passing me by
Letting go before I am even a thought
A steady path of abandonment
Leading me with deception
With the cruel lie of their love
Only to drop me into the wind
Apathetic to where I would land

Kearsen Danielle

Empty hands that fled too quickly
Silence rolling off your tongue
Torture trapped within your eyes
Every glance bearing a million swords

You could never love me
No matter how hard you tried
I was only ever a reminder
Of the worst day of your life

Journey to Healing

Abandon me
Kiss me while I sleep
A packed bag sliding over your chest
Pressing into the bed
Too often these steps are carved
So leave with no regrets
Whisper your goodbye
While the love goes dead

Kearsen Danielle

I bleed for you
As you make my body weak
Kissing your knuckles
Just before they graze my cheek

I could see it in your eyes
The way the dark clouds circled
Hungry for domination

It was always more than verbal
　So light a cigarette
　　Put the fire on my skin
　　　Pull the ropes tight
　　　　So that you're sure to win

Journey to Healing

Running around your finger
Tiptoeing across eggshells
Whatever you wanted
I did

I would've jumped off the bridge
And in return
You mock my every move
Laughing at every tear that falls
Disappearing for days at a time
Leaving me waiting by the phone
Hoping to hear just one word
Any word that you'll come home

But it wasn't to be
The constant manipulation that ruled me
How the abuse commanded my mind
Tricking me to believe your heinous lies
Fearing anything that was actually good
All because I thought it was true love

But it never was…

…was it?

Kearsen Danielle

Here we are
Lying cold on the floor
Hoping for heat to rise between us

Heat that never comes

Instead our bodies start to freeze
Our hearts numbing with every dropping degree

Maybe eventually
We will learn
Some things are not meant to be
Some people fight when it's better to leave

Journey to Healing

Are we here again
   Have we come back to this place of pain
    This place is too familiar to me
    Your arms drag me back to my seat
    You've etched my name on it clearly
    Did I ever really leave

Why are we here again
   It's raining
   But the drops aren't rain
   They're our tears of the past
   There's a storm
   And the thunder echoes from my fists
   The lightning smacks across your face
   Your words flying across the sky
   Scratching at my skin
   Picking me apart
   Every word
   Every promise
   Every lie

We're here again
   It's the same
   And it's different
   The rumbling charges beneath my feet
   A low growl threatening to break through
   Cracks flowing like a sea of glass
   My heart isn't beating like it should
   It's more of a slow drum
   Each hit flooding my body
   Widening the cuts along my soul

You're here again
   Standing next to a limp body
   A body full of scars and bruises

Simply a wounded vessel
Healed breaks reflecting twice as many fresh
With no limbs to move or heart to live
I know you don't recognize it
Recognize me
So you leave
Unbeknownst that you caused this

I'm here again
With no strength to move
No heart to feel
The storm swallows me whole
Lifting every piece into its atmosphere
Leaving me stuck in the eye
Each one slipping through my fingers
Forever out of reach
Forever beyond me

Journey to Healing

Words reaching through the walls
Voices at war with one another
Breaking things in their path
Of all the mistakes made
Of all the fights hashed
This was the worst of all

Heartache echoing from our bodies
Radiating throughout the room
Lighting a fire between the two
An emotional fire feasting on our fears
Devouring each and every tear
Consuming any love that remained
Until there was nothing left but the pain

Kearsen Danielle

Sometimes I try to imagine it
The many thoughts that ran through your head
Your fingers running along her body
The words that left your lips
How your eyes gazed upon her
As you tied yourself to another

It hurts
More than I care to admit
The unbearable truth of not knowing
Of not understanding what you did

Was I not enough for you?
Could I not satisfy all that you were?
Were you trapped in this life,
One you didn't ask for?

I try to imagine
But instead
I'm left more broken than before

Journey to Healing

I was constantly alone
Your body stood in front of me
But you were nowhere to be found

Consumed by her every word
I sought comfort in something new
Diving into the drinks that whispered my name

Temporary peace sat in the blur
The lack of sensation that overcame
Every night walking the edge of a glass
Ready to plunge into its abyss
Praying for you to save me
Wondering if I'd even be missed

And when the nights would arrive
It would hang on my breath
As you decided
                it
                    wasn't
                        worth
                            notice.

Kearsen Danielle

I thought I was beyond it
    The moments of wondering why
    Thinking of your hands
    Roaming each night
    How you must've felt as you accomplished your lie
    The words flowed too easily
    Too freely
    Too well

I thought I was beyond it
    And yet I asked myself
    Was this the first time
    Why couldn't I tell
    Did I miss the signs
    Because they seem clear as day
    And yet I continued on
    Believing we were fine

Maybe I just made it up in my mind

I thought I was beyond it
    And clearly I'm not
    I thought I could forget it
    But I'm just left distraught

Journey to Healing

I've forgiven you
Of course I have
But how do I say that I can't forget
That I trust you

But sometimes there are these moments
I see it play again

    Moments.

Where I wonder if it replays in your head

    Moments.

Fear whispers what if it happens again

Kearsen Danielle

Hearing the silence come from within
Everything changed
In an instant you were gone
And along went my heart
Every piece of who I was
Not an ounce left behind
And I knew right then
I would never be the same
I would never hear your cry

So I let myself fall
Knowing I couldn't have stopped it anyways
Because I'd never know you
The sound of your laugh
The look of your face
The light in your eyes
I wouldn't get the chance to hold you
Not even for a night

Journey to Healing

Empty cribs
Broken dreams
Empty hearts
Broken beings

Never would I have thought
I'd leave without you in my arms
What did I do to make this happen
Where did I go wrong
Could I have prevented this
And been a better mom

Kearsen Danielle

BEAUTY IN ASHES

Journey to Healing

Standing here
I'm unable to see any relief
Burdened by the pain in my body

"I am with you"

You say
Reaching to hold me
Bringing me to my knees

I'm trying to believe
To see past
What's in front of me

And as I cry out
So gently
You speak

"There is hope in me"

Psalm 39:7

Kearsen Danielle

As I fall through this glass floor
Begging to grasp just one piece
Being torn apart by every sharp edge

I refuse You again

Even as the blood pours from my wounds
As my body becomes limp
And I'm losing my grip

I refuse You again

And as my fingers finally slip
I plummet below toward the abyss
Prepared for the emptiness
Only to fall into Your arms

Because while I refused to accept You
You heard my cries and loved me all along
You were by my side every moment
And in my weakness you were strong

2 Corinthians 12:9

Journey to Healing

I want more than the darkness that surrounds
Beating me down
Scared of what it would take to heal
But more so of the hurt that strives to kill

Exhausted from the numbness that really isn't numb
But instead an endless void
Driving me to the furthest corner of my mind
Silencing my voice

Careless and empty
A shell dangling along in life
Barely holding any desire to feel
Or fight

Abandoned and alone
Rejected by every home that could've been
And every love I hoped would be
I struggle with this light sitting in front of me

Something new and unknown
Promising things I've only ever hoped
Hands stretching to take my own
Lifting me out of the pain I called my home

Showing me there is more to life
Healing and peace
Someone to fight not just *with* me
But *for* me

Someone willing to take up the sword
To be my shield
To comfort me
And help me heal

Kearsen Danielle

And with the fear
I'll take His hand
To rise into
A newfound land

Psalm 56:3

Journey to Healing

Broken down to my final breath
Scraping to hold onto life
Even with all the blood I lost
I fought against them
No matter the hits endured
I couldn't let them win

And when I was ready to say goodbye
God told me it was not the end

He became my feet
To help me stand
He became my strength
Though I was condemned

When they came against me
He came to my defense
And now today
I am loved by Him

Psalm 94:22

Kearsen Danielle

When the dark becomes overwhelming
My soul
      Aching
            Slowly being crushed

I begin to wonder if this is my life now
A shell of who I was
Or hoped to be

A person
Merely surviving

And when another piece breaks
You place Your hands on my soul
Holding together every shattered part
Comforting every tear that threatens to fall
Loving me as no one has before
So now I lay down my all
I give it to You
Lord

Psalm 56:8

Sitting here
I find myself broken and alone
Bruised by the hands that surround me
And the words that leave their tongues

I am never enough for them
I'll never receive their love
I will always be an outcast
Something they'd rather be rid of

And when I cry out
Praying for one who'd never leave
I look up as You say

"Give your all to me"

Deuteronomy 4:29

Kearsen Danielle

Doubt creeps among my thoughts
Strength failing ever so swiftly
Causing echoes to engulf me

I cannot hear anyone
Or anything
Constantly fighting
Running
From the unbelief

I know that He is with me
Even when all seems quiet
I must reach out my hand to trust Him
Before the sounds of the world riot
Giving all I have
All I am
And all I'll ever be
To the One who knows my heart
And is always with me

Psalm 139:23

Thorns tear at my sides
Scratching to open every wound
Though the spines cut into me
My eyes are opened to see You clearly
I am brought to my knees
Every time
Calling upon Your name
My flesh is too weak in this moment
I ask for Your strength

Just enough to make it through
Lord
My body aches
Cold and weary in Your midst
Please
I need a break
Your hands bring relief again
Helping me escape
I am forever grateful
Crying out my thanks

Isaiah 14:3

Kearsen Danielle

This trial is too much
Kicking me on the ground
Covering my eyes with the dirt of the world
An attempt to blind and deceive
To steal my blessings

Yet the enemy forgets
God is in control
He turns it all around
Washing away the old
Clearing my sight
Holding my hand
Lifting me up
Helping me stand

I am not alone
This trial is not too much
For my God is bigger
And so is His love

Psalm 73:26

Journey to Healing

I build this house
Again and again
Only to watch it fall
Sinking beneath the sand
Every part crumbling before my eyes
Weak against the weight of this world

The cracks begin to reflect on my heart
Bringing a dull ache to my being
To the foundations of what is built
Of all that is me

Then His voice whispers
Sweetly through the wind
His breath begins to carry away the pieces
All to place me upon solid ground
A ground I've never been

As this house is built once more
Nerves run their course upon my skin
Only this time
I am not on sinking sand

Isaiah 33:6

54

Kearsen Danielle

Being left alone
Forgotten
And unknown
Ruins my self worth
With mistrust down to the bone
My beliefs of love waver
For I've never had a home
A place to accept the person I am
Instead I'm left to roam
Upon this dry and desert land

When I found the Lord
I was hesitant to believe
That I could be loved
Unconditionally

And since He placed His hand
Upon my weary head
I've only ever known
The truth of what He's said

Isaiah 55:11

Journey to Healing

I sit here
Wondering how everything got so bad
How I could've lost myself so easily
Broken and shattered
Not just in my heart
But through my entire being

The pain was too much to bear alone

Don't you see
I forget His word sometimes
The One that gave me His commands
He said not to fight alone
But to fight hand in hand
Because without the Lord
I constantly drown
Deeper to the sea's depths
Choking on every struggle found

But if I am willing
If I take His hand
He'll pull me above the water
And I will finally stand

Isaiah 41:10

Kearsen Danielle

Every scar running miles wide
Etched along my soul
Leaving space for the world
I sat vulnerable

Unable to move
Slowly losing myself
Breaking apart with every person
And all the lies they dealt

It wasn't until
I saw His hand
Felt His strength
Lifting me again

Filling every crack with His love
Sealing every trench with His peace
I am made whole through the Lord
With Him I can finally see

1 Thessalonians 5:23-24

Journey to Healing

Reaching out to touch Your robe
Hoping for Your peace
Praying for Your love
Only You can deliver me
Save me from the mess I've become

Oh Lord
I cry out
Giving You all I am
I pray
For Your merciful hand

1 Chronicles 21:13

Kearsen Danielle

Every step I take
Cutting like knives
Scarring the bottom of my feet
Burning their hatred into my skin
The farther I go
The harder it is to breathe

Still I will continue
As His love holds serenity
The sacred peace I long for
The ability to be set free
So on I will go
To find the One
I wholly seek

Philippians 4:6-7

Without a care in the world
I slip into the streets
Silently hoping for it to be the last time
Consuming every bottle I could find
Thinking it would fill this void
The emptiness inside of me
Handfuls of pills on repeat
Yet nothing was able to numb the space

I waited for death to come to my door
Only to be drawn to my knees
Letting my pain go at the altar

I never knew love before this

I had given up that it would ever exist
But God laid His hands on me
Bringing about a new person completely
A person I never thought I could be
Someone healed and whole
Someone worth loving

2 Corinthians 5:17

Kearsen Danielle

I bow at Your feet
With arms open wide
My soul deeply scarred

I know to believe in You
Is to breathe again
Yet I can't help but fear I've failed

For years I've come and gone
Calling whenever I see fit
Not willing to put in the time
To fully commit

Slowly I've come to realize
I must give You my whole heart
My whole self
And place into Your hands
Before this peace can start

So I lay down before You now
Praying that You hear
For in Your arms
I hope to be found
To have You
Always near

James 4:8

Journey to Healing

There were bricks in my throat
Put there by the very ones who 'love' me
Every word I tried to breathe laced with cement
My hands tied to the fence
The ropes burning their words into my skin

I just wanted to be loved.

I tried to cough up the pieces
Every time getting shoved to the ground
I tried to give in and let go
To conform to your desires
But I couldn't handle the pressure

I just wanted to be loved.

They painted my eyes with their story
Drilled holes in my head to bury me
The weight held my thoughts captive
No matter how far I got
My soul couldn't escape

I just wanted to be loved.

I could hear the anger rolling off their lips in the quiet
Every threat echoing in my dreams
Chasing me till the morning
Scratching away at every smile
Stealing the peace from my essence

I just wanted to be loved.

Until You entered through the door
Pulling me from the ground
You untied every knot sewn in my skin

Kearsen Danielle

Every crack lining my heart
Filling my being with hope

Could you ever love me?

I am no longer a mere body
But a soul set free
I am weightless
Soaring high over the seas
With Your hand in mine
Every fear wiped clean
You saved my life
You gave me liberty

Oh, how you perfectly love me.

Psalm 18:48

Journey to Healing

As I walk this path
The wind pushes against me
Causing my body to start deteriorating
Each step leading to more dust
My head telling me to stop
And my heart begging me to go on
With a war raging inside
I lose more life
Breezes turning to storms
Blowing away my soul

Or so I thought

But it is not my soul that's blown away
It is everything that surrounds
Each piece dissipating before my eyes
And just like that
The storm is gone
Along with the person I was
Leaving a new body in its place
With a new path carved before my feet
I can only imagine
Where it will lead

Romans 6:6

Kearsen Danielle

BLOSSOMED BRANCHES

I am a branch
  Severed
  Removed
  Never fitting the mold of others
  Or finding a tree with room

I am a branch
  And I cannot try
  To fit in anymore
  I cannot hide
  Or be what they ask for

So instead of looking
  To attach myself
  I'll let my leaves bloom
  And allow the wind
  To guide me someplace new

For when my seeds sprout
  I will rise once again
  I'll finally fit in
  My own tree
  Full of love
  And bearing fruit

Psalm 1:3

Kearsen Danielle

Slowly flowing through your hair
Gently kissing every inch of skin
Dancing across this field full of beauty
Holding every dream in His hand
A surreal life of peace hiding between the trees
Are you ready
To feel His breeze

John 14:27

Journey to Healing

A simple touch
Of His hands
Snapping my soul awake
Breaking off
Every old branch
And lighting up my face

I've never had such joy as this
Or known what love felt like
I never had a hunger
For His will
And His light

But now it fills my heart
To be close to Him
To listen to His words
And live according to them

I thought it would be hard
Letting worldly things go
But as they left
I noticed
All the pain started to slow

My mind finding ease
Even in the night
Once again
I can think
I can breathe
I can fight

Only by His strength
By His will
And His might

Kearsen Danielle

I am forever grateful
To be called a child of light

Ephesians 5:8

Journey to Healing

Lord I praise You
Till the end of my time
I strive to tell the world
Of Your beautiful design
How precious life can be
If they would open up their eyes
And seek You Lord
With all of their lives

Ecclesiastes 3:11

Kearsen Danielle

Steadily I stand on this ground
As the arrows fly over my head
My enemies strive
To pierce my heart
Wanting me all but dead

I will not fear
No matter what
For I know God stands with me
He shields me from the wicked
And pierces them instead

Deuteronomy 28:7

You showed me a love
    Unlike any I've known
    Unconditional
    And true
    Becoming my home

You proved this love
    Time and time again
    Standing by my side
    Holding up my hand

You showed me real joy
    How to smile
    How to laugh
    You showed me
    Deep comfort
    And all I had to do was ask

Your voice spoke above
    And I could finally see
    All your hand created
    Even
    All of me

Ephesians 2:10

Kearsen Danielle

Mountains rising into the sky
Standing so beautifully
Before my eyes
How the valleys dip
Under the light
Weaving through
The rocks at night

Wherever I am
He lifts me up
Surrounding me
With His unfailing love

Jeremiah 31:3

As we lay wrapped together
Beneath the sheets
I look upon your face
Unable to contain the laugh
Erupting from my chest
The brightest light
Shining from your eyes
As your smile matches mine
A fit of laughter filling the room
A joy neither of us ever knew
Planted deep in our souls
The depths changing
Everything that we know
Creating joy in every moment
Filling us with love
Revealing the beauty
Given from above

Romans 5:5

Kearsen Danielle

Oh Daughter
    My precious creation
    The beauty you contain is immense
    The gentle flow of your hair
    Falling against your skin

Oh Daughter
    How your eyes shine like the stars I made
    A smile that brings light upon the dark
    Each part so beautiful
    All to make up who you are

Oh Daughter
    Don't be fooled by what the world speaks
    What the numbers display
    For you were made by me
    I made every person
    So beautiful and intricate
    I have made you in my image

Or did you forget?

Genesis 1:27

Journey to Healing

Tears follow behind another
Steady on this track along my face
Running ever so quickly
Except they're so different from before

Filled not with numbness and pain
But with a love so pure

An overwhelming sense of gratitude
For the One that saved my soul
The One that dug me out of this hole
Renewing me completely
Restoring me so beautifully

So I let the tears fall
For these tears are for the Lord
As I will never again crawl
But will forever stand tall

Psalm 46:5

Kearsen Danielle

The one who placed the stars into motion
Counting each by name instead of number
Recognizing its beautiful light
Reflecting from Your splendor

Everything of this world
Known and designed by Your hands
To know each creation by name
To have such an intricate plan

How small I am compared to it all
Yet You hold me in Your arms
You are my Shield and Protector
Saving me from harm

And still through every day and night
I am forever seen
A beautiful thing it is
To be known by the Great Almighty

Psalm 147:4

Journey to Healing

Small feet running through the yard
Anxious to catch every firefly among the stars
Serotonin levels running high
Strong arms hugging me from behind
All I could ever want
Finally at reach
A life of peace and family
All I'll ever need

Psalm 128

Kearsen Danielle

I hear your heart beating
Staying on a steady rhythm
Drumming against my own
Your cry echoes through the room
Breaking my chest wide open
Eyes releasing a waterfall

I am mesmerized by your beauty
So grateful to the One above
For my soul floods with abounding love

The intoxicating smell of a precious life
Filling the room with a glowing light
God blessed me with you
My beautiful joy
My sweet, sweet, sweet boy

John 16:21

Journey to Healing

I watch you sometimes
The way you move so effortlessly
Every strand of hair flowing with the wind
Gliding easily within your movements
Before falling into place on command
The light coming from your eyes
Holds a thousand fireflies
Glowing through the night
They fly below the stars
Singing softly to each other
Your laugh drums in my chest
Threatening to break the skin
Every smile setting my soul free
Leaving me frozen
Wanting for a second longer
Just a moment to pause your beauty
To breathe in how precious you are
For you are the joy God gave me

Psalm 127:3

Kearsen Danielle

No fear will stand a chance

    When God stands with us

Nothing can stand against

    For He is mighty and righteous

John 16:33

I stand to tell God's truth
To share of His incredible love
Great faithfulness
His strength
And abundance

The words of others won't matter
Because I know
What His words say

God calls me chosen
  Forgiven
    Adopted
      And redeemed

Wife
  Daughter
    Worthy
      And Belonging

Healed with just a breath
  Heard
    Known
      And seen

He calls me heir
  Sheep
    Accepted
      Masterpiece

Anointed
  Warrior
    Light
      Beauty

Kearsen Danielle

Created for a purpose
  Renewed
    Beloved
      Set free

This is what He says of me

Matthew 22:14

I'm a child of God
Standing
Spreading
Speaking
Unsheathing the sword

His love
Embracing
Engulfing
Elevating
Forgiving forevermore

Word after word
A wildfire
Lighting every crevice
Burning away the old

Rising
　　From the ashes
　　　Of the world

Isaiah 61:3

Kearsen Danielle

Carry me with Your wings
Lift me above the ground
Remove every stone upon me
Every weight holding me down
Take my soul into Your hands
Let Your presence surround
Carry me with Your wings
For I am finally found

Psalm 91:4

I give thanks to the Lord
For His beautiful voice
The voice of love and guidance
Quieting the noise

I give thanks to the Lord
For each of you here
For every word you took
I pray it was clear

May God begin to heal
Any wounded soul
With the incredible power
Only the One above holds

In Jesus name
Amen

Psalm 18:6

Thank you for taking the time to read this book. I pray you were able to receive some hope and strength to approach your own healing with the Lord. Although it can be hard to face your pain, it is worth it. Healing is real and possible for you.

And I hope that through this, you found even a little bit of faith, a mustard-seed worth. Because faith truly does move mountains.

If you have but a mustard seed worth of faith, nothing shall be impossible for you.
Matthew 17:20

Biblical Affirmations

He loved you from the beginning.
1 John 4:19

God hears you and heals you.
Psalm 30:2

He loves you so much that He gave His only son.
John 3:16

God said it will be done by your faith.
Matthew 9:29

Believe that you will be whole and He will heal you.
Mark 5:28-29

Believe in Jesus and you will be saved.
Acts 16:31

He will give you strength.
Isaiah 40:29

God heals your heart and wounds.
Psalm 147:3

He hears you and sees your tears; He will heal you.
2 Kings 20:5

God will do it for you.
Jeremiah 17:14

He loves you and will help you.

Romans 8:28

He died so you could live and be healed.
1 Peter 2:24

God rescues you from death.
Psalm 107:20

You are forgiven.
James 5:15

He is always with you, and He will strengthen you.
Isaiah 41:10

He forgives your sins and heals you.
Psalm 103:3

The Lord will restore you.
Jeremiah 30:17

God gives you rest.
Matthew 11:28

Seek Him and He will give these things to you.
Matthew 6:33

He will do more than you can think or imagine.
Ephesians 3:20

Take every worry to Him.
Philippians 4:6

Your faith in Him heals you. Have peace and be free.
Mark 5:34

I pray you have health and prosperity.
3 John 1:2

About the Author

Kearsen Danielle is a poet, author, singer/songwriter, and follower of Christ who writes about mental health, hope, strength, faith, and more.

She has a Bachelor's in Communication and Media from Florida State College of Jacksonville.

Her debut poetry collection, *Surviving*, was re-released in April 2025. This collection focuses on helping you find God's strength to make it through life's struggles.

Her second poetry collection, *Journey to Healing*, was also re-released in April 2025. This collection was written for when you're in need of God's peace and healing.

When Kearsen is not writing, she is fishing with her family, working on her to-be-read list, or having conversations with someone about Christ.

Kearsen pens a monthly newsletter about books, words from God, encouragement, updates, and more. Follow along @kearsendanielle on Instagram and Facebook or kearsendanielle.com for more.